The Beautiful Beans

Annabel Townsend

ISBN-13: 978-1481049313

TO
MUM AND DAD

For all your help with The Big Move and for supporting all my coffee dreams.

CONTENTS

ACKNOWLEDGMENTS

This book came about through National Novel Writing Month ('Nanowrimo') 2012. I was originally writing some high-speed novel about time-traveling bicycles, but despite my best efforts it just didn't happen for me this year. So I decided to go back to what I know and love, Coffee. This is the result. Despite the failure of my novel, I met some wonderful, creative and talented people during the month of novelling madness and thank them all for their company, encouragement and the eccentric yet creative environment they generate as a collective.

Thank you also to my fellow coffee geeks, baristas and co-workers, Tamara, Taneille, Mike, Dave, Sarah and Trevor, who have put up with me waffling on about my books and novel writing for far too long. Some of their coffee efforts appear in this book, so I also thank them for their patience as I carefully took photographs of their drinks before they served them!

The writing of this book would not have been possible without the help of Carolina, who has patiently kept my daughter occupied and happy at her wonderful daycare, and thus prevented her from helping me type, (please see my Nanowrimo Attempt in 2010 to see why this was an absolute necessity!)

Finally, I am eternally grateful for the support and enthusiasm from my husband Carl, whose taste in coffee is now quite discerning, and for my daughter Miranda, who will happily drink espresso whenever we let her.

1 MYTHS AND LEGENDS

"Coffee, the finest organic suspension ever devised."

~Star Trek: Voyager

1 MYTHS AND LEGENDS

It all started with a goat.

Probably not one like that. That one lives on a farm in Hertfordshire, UK.

The goat in question supposedly lived in ancient Abyssinia (Ethiopia) in the ninth century.

Legend has it that coffee – or at least, the coffee plant, was discovered by accident by a young goatherd called Kaldi, who was idly watching his flock in the Abyssinian bush. He became concerned when some of the goats began braying loudly and dancing about madly and excitedly. They appeared to be chewing the berries off a small shrub with dark green leaves and small, bright red fruit. Presumably the dancing was a result of the world's first caffeine rush.

Kaldi took some of the curious berries to the local Imam to find out why his goats were acting so strangely after eating them. The Imam immediately assumed that the berries were the work of Satan, designed to tempt and intoxicate, and so threw them into the fire. The berries roasted in the flames and released such an amazing aroma that the Imam realised that the berries could not possibly be an evil thing, instead they smelled so good they must be a gift from God himself!

This story never goes on to say whether Kaldi, or even the goats were ever given any recognition for their monumental discovery. We do not speak of "having a cup of Kaldi", for instance. The word "coffee" may be a derivative of "Kaffa" which is an area in Southwestern Ethiopia where the plant grows in the wild. However, it is more likely to have come from the Arabic name "Qahweh", which originally referred to a type of wine. In seventeenth century Europe, coffee was known as the "wine of the Arabs" as they did not drink alcohol. The Ottoman Turkish traders then turned the word into "Kahve", which in turn has been corrupted into *Caffe* in Italian, *Cafe* in Spanish and French and *Coffee* in English.

But back to Kaldi and the goats. There is absolutely no way of knowing if there is one iota of truth in this legend of course, but it endures partially because it is the sort of story that many would like to be true. There are now many, many coffee companies who use imagery of dancing goats or use the name Kaldi in their branding, and so our unlikely hero lives on.

Brazil is the largest producer of coffee in the world, and Colombia comes in third place after Vietnam. There are various myths about how coffee came to be cultivated in Latin America in the first place. The most common and most romantic is the story of Gabriel Mathieu de Clieu. De Clieu was a French naval officer, serving in the French colonies in Martinique. Whilst on leave in Paris in 1720, he allegedly had an affair with the French governor's wife, who, as a parting gift, gave him a bouquet of flowers with a small coffee sapling hidden in the middle. De Clieu managed to keep the coffee plant alive all the way back to Martinique by sacrificing part of his own water supply on board the ship to feed it. Miraculously, it survived and was replanted, and thrived. By 1776 Martinique's first commercial coffee harvest was ready, with every plant having stemmed from that one sapling in the bouquet.

There has always been a variety of myths surrounding the health benefits – or concerns – of coffee drinking. The first complaint against the drink dates back to the 17th Century, when women petitioned against the coffee houses that were 'stealing away' their husbands!

"the Excessive use of that Newfangled, Abominable, Heathenish Liquor called COFFEE, which Riffling Nature of her Choicest Treasures, and Drying up the Radical Moisture, has so Eunucht our Husbands, and Crippled our more kind Gallants, that they are become as Impotent, as Age, and as unfruitful as those Desarts whence that unhappy Berry is said to be brought."
(1674, in Brandon 2007).

Nowadays, we know coffee doesn't make men impotent, but its active ingredient, caffeine, has been blamed for causing everything from hypertension and heart palpitations to osteoporosis and, of course, insomnia. Conversely, it is also supposed to ward off the onset of dementia and Alzheimer's disease (particularly in women), is thought to prevent bowel cancer in men, and may also be a natural antidepressant. Either way, it is the most widely consumed legal stimulant in the world and people have apparently been enjoying it since the ninth century!

Even the names of some of the different coffee drinks arose from the realms of legend.

A **Mocha**, for example, is espresso mixed with chocolate and topped up with foamed milk. The name comes from the Yemeni port of Mocha from where coffee was traded around the world in the fifteenth and sixteenth centuries, but ironically the people of Mocha actually used to believe that adding milk to your coffee would give you leprosy.

'**Latte**' just means 'milk' in Italian, but be sure to pronounce it "Lah-tay" not "Lar-tay", because Lar-tay is Scillian slang for "circumcision"....

During the Second World War, many American troops stationed in Italy found the traditional Italian espresso far too strong, so they diluted it with more hot water, and the "**Americano**" was born.

Finally, a **Cappuccino**, (espresso with thick, dense milk foam) was apparently named after the Capuchin monks who shaved their tonsures. The circle of brown espresso with a mound of white milk foam in the centre was supposed to look like the top of a monk's head!

2 COFFEE'S GLOBAL HISTORY

Last comes the beverage of the Orient shore,

Mocha, far off, the fragrant berries bore.

Taste the dark fluid with a dainty lip,

Digestion waits on pleasure as you sip.

~Pope Leo XII

2 COFFEE'S GLOBAL HISTORY

The spread of coffee around the globe

Most sources agree that coffee was brought from Ethiopia and Sudan along with slaves, to Yemen and then throughout Arabia. Coffee was being cultivated in Yemen from the 15th century onwards, and exported through the port of Mocha. It became known as the 'wine of the Arabs', who adopted the drink for its energy giving properties, allowing priests to pray longer into the night and still be able to concentrate. Although the authorities frequently tried to ban it, coffee houses spread throughout the Arab world.

To Europe

Coffee was first brought to Europe (via Mocha) by Venetian traders in 1615, where it was sold primarily as a form of medicine. The first coffee house in Europe opened in Venice in 1683. Londoners also adopted coffee very quickly as social centres. The drink proved extremely popular and Edward Lloyd opened his coffee house in 1688, which was populated mainly by merchants. This coffee house later became Lloyds of London, the insurance company.

To the Far East

The Dutch East Indies company, also buying coffee plants from Mocha, began to cultivate coffee in Malabar in India, and then, in 1699, founded the first plantations in Java, Indonesia. The Dutch became the biggest suppliers of coffee to Europe, and Indonesia remains the fourth largest producer of coffee in the world.

To the Americas

Coffee shops were established in North America by the end of 17th century, and the Boston Tea Party, where Americans demonstrated their rejection of English rule and taxation by dumping tea shipments into the harbour, was planned in a coffee house called the Green Dragon, in 1773. Coffee then became the drink of choice in North America.

Gabriel Mathieu de Clieu may have brought coffee to Martinique, but the Dutch also brought coffee to their colonies in Surinam, and then to French Guyana and later, to huge plantations in Brazil. The British also brought some to Jamaica, where the most expensive coffee in the world, Blue Mountain coffee, is still produced. By 1820, there were coffee plantations all over Latin America, and the crop became extremely important to the economy of the entire region.

To England:

Coffee first reached London in around 1650 and became extremely popular, with coffee houses offering an alternative to taverns. Most were laid out with a coffee bar at one end (but plenty of waitresses often of dubious reputation!) and long benches to sit at, forcing strangers to sit next to each other. Unsurprisingly, this led to a breaking down of rank and social hierarchy if only within the coffee house, and people, well, men, began "free and open debates" – or in other words, plenty of informed but caffeinated arguing. It is a fairly well known legend that Lloyds of London started out as a coffee shop, with merchants meeting in it to conduct their trades. But there were other now famous institutions that also had coffee origins. Coffee houses in different places had particular themes – the ones around the theatres attracted the 'wits' and critics and poets and so on, the coffee shops near the printers were filled with the pamphleteers and the ones near the schools were where they scientists hung out. The Royal Society was originally founded by three men who met and formed "The Chemical Club" in a coffee shop in Oxford, and they'd perform scientific experiments in public in the coffee shops.

> "In the coffee houses men of science, learning and scholarship found they had unprecedented access to all kinds of knowledge: commercial, literary, mechanical, theological. Unlike the narrow confines of the Schools, whether university, church or club, the coffee house opened the whole world of learning to the clientele. To a seventeenth century mind, entering a coffee house was like walking into the internet." (Ellis, 2004)

And so, the Penny University was born. As well as being referred to by coffee fans as 'penny universities' or "the free school of ingenuity", they were also called by their critics "a poseur's paradise." Nothing changes. Many people nowadays, myself included still sit in coffee shops for hours, now equipped with laptops but still attempting to look intellectual. We just use internet forums to rant on rather than striking up conversation with anyone else in the room, which is quite sad really. Some things that have changed for the better are a.) the coffee and b) the clientele.

This was a long time before espresso machines and even before anyone thought to filter the stuff. The coffee in 1670's London was at best, Turkish style, as in, roasted in a pan over a fire, ground up roughly then boiled in water, thus improving the safety of the water but often producing a drink that looked, smelled and tasted like soot. And quite possibly cut with charcoaled weevil, since it was transported from the colonies by boat. Also, the coffee houses were exclusively populated by men. Women could serve in them but did not attend and were not privy to the cheap education on offer there. Somewhat bizarrely though, they were allowed to own them. The most famous coffeehouse madam was Moll King, and King's Coffee House was extremely popular but not necessarily because of her coffee....

There were other similarities to modern universities too:

> *"in we went, where a packet of muddling muckworms were busy as so many rats in an old cheese-loft, some going, some coming, some scribbling, some talking, some drinking,...and the whole room stinking of tobacco like a dutch barge or a boatswain's cabin."*

Now, doesn't that sound like undergraduate halls of residence?

I wrote my PhD thesis about the coffee industry, and did most of the writing on my laptop whilst sitting in different coffee shops. For nearly four years as a postgrad student, this was what my "coffice" looked like!

3 THE LIFE CYCLE OF A COFFEE PLANT

"Desde el campo, viene la calidad."

('From the countryside, comes the quality')

- Alfredo, Nicaraguan Coffee Farmer

3 THE LIFE CYCLE OF A COFFEE PLANT

Arabica coffee grows at high altitude in tropical cloudforest. This is in Northern Nicaragua

Farmers build little coffee nurseries to protect the delicate saplings

Small plants are then planted out amongst the forest. They will not produce coffee fruit until they are 3-4 years old.

Coffee crops can get quite dense!

At first, the fruit is hard and greenish yellow, before it ripens.

Other taller plants and trees shade the coffee crop so that ripening happens slowly, which Improves the coffee's flavour.

One coffee tree only produces 1-2lb of cherries a year

Eventually, the berries (called Cherries) ripen to a deep red, and are all picked by hand.

After the fruit has been picked and the harvest is over, the tree flowers to produce next year's crop

The finished coffee from bean to cup.

4 FARM LIFE

No one can understand the truth

until he drinks of coffee's frothy goodness.

~Sheik Abd-al-Kadir

4 FARM LIFE

Coffee farming is a family business, and everyone has a role, from picking the cherries to sorting the beans

Two-thirds of the coffee farms in Nicaragua are less than 2 hectares in size.

Small farms often work together in much larger cooperatives to sell their coffee.

Around 25 million people are employed in producing coffee around the world.

Picking beans is hard work, but all the ripe cherries have to be picked as soon as possible. The harvest season in Central America is only a few short weeks in November and December

The fruit is removed from the beans using a "depulper" machine, which is handcranked and simply squashed the hard beans out of the soft fruit.

Beans are then washed in cold water to remove the sticky sweet muscelage that attached them to the fruit.

Then the beans are left to dry in the sun

Next, all the beans are sorted: picking out broken, discoloured, misshapen or mouldy beans or those infected with weevils. This is a very meticulous, time-consuming process! (and not really done by the kids!)

The sorted beans are then bagged up...

..and then transported to the cooperative's processing plant - by any means necessary! (in this case, standing on the back of a neighbour's truck also delivering bananas)

After leaving the farm, the beans are taken to a central processing mill, called a 'Beneficio' where beans from hundreds of small farms are all collected together for grading, trade and export.

The beans are dried out further by spreading them out on a concrete patio in the hot sun. People are employed to walk up and down the patios turning the beans over with a rake, so that they dry evenly.

Then they are sorted again by a complex and intricate machine called an "Oliver", which automatically sorts coffee by size, shape, density, colour and weight. This helps to ensure the highest quality standards, so that the farmers get the highest price possible for their crop.

Processing coffee effectively is an extremely long and complicated process and require considerable knowledge and skill, and the process doesn't just end on the farm.

The 22 Steps of Coffee Production

On Farm Stages

1. Growth and maintenance to fruit-bearing age

2. Flowering/Budding/Ripening

3. Picking

4. Water sorting

5. Fermentation

6. Depulping

7. Washing

8. Partial drying

9. Sorting

10. Grading

11. Full drying/turning

12. Trilling/deparchment

13. Full sorting

Trade and Roasting Stages

14. Cupping

15. Export/Certification/Shipping

16. Roasting

17. Blending

In Cafe Stages

8. Grinding

19. Dosing

20. Tamping

21. Brewing

22. Serving

5 MIGHTY MACHINES

I believe humans get a lot done, not because we're smart,

but because we have thumbs so we can make coffee.

~Flash Rosenberg

5 MIGHTY MACHINES

Coffee is not produced just through human labour, there are many machines that help turn the little hard green beans into delicious drinks as well.
Machinery used on coffee farms bears little resemblance to the technology found in coffee shops:

Despite the technology, it can still be very hands-on work!

Coffee roasters come in all shapes and sizes....

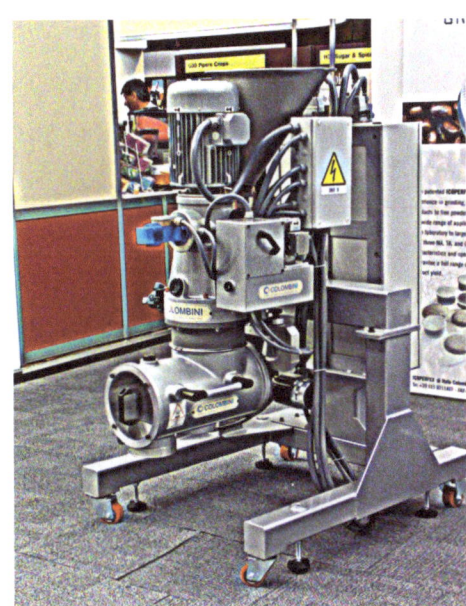

Grinding the coffee is not as simple as it sounds. Different methods of brewing the coffee, (and different machines to brew it with) require different styles of grinds. It all depends on how long the coffee spends in contact with water. Imagine a jar of pebbles and a jar of sand. Water poured on to the sand will take longer to filter through than when it is poured through the pebbles.

An espresso machine pushes water on to the coffee for only twenty to thirty seconds. Therefore, ground coffee for espresso machines needs to be like sand (or finer!) so that the water pressed through it has time to extract as much coffee goodness as possible. Coarser grinds are used for percolated or filtered coffee, which can be brewed for up to five minutes.

This is also why espresso tastes so distinctively different from brewed coffee.

Coffee is transported from farms to roasters to coffee shops or people's homes by any means possible! This is a traditional Costa Rican coffee cart, used for moving raw beans from rural coffee plantations to the big cities ready for export. The carts were always brightly coloured and highly decorative and would have been pulled by donkeys.

Clockwise from below left: Costa Rican 'sock' filter; Turkish Ibrik; Pour over filter; French Press/ Cafetiere; Siphon pot and Aeropress; Gaggia Espresso machine; Clover machine and Elektra La Belle Epoque steam-espresso maker

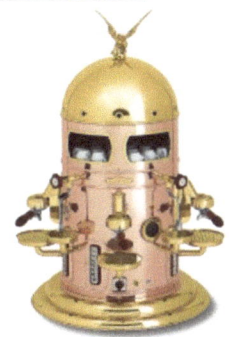

Espresso is not the only method of brewing coffee, and making a good brew does not aways require complicated and expensive technology!

6 ROASTING TO PERFECTION

Good coffee may come from Arabia or India, from the Blue Mountains of Jamaica, or via France with an a mixture of chicory; but its flavor and excellence will be derived from daily careful roasting and grinding, a truism universally admitted and habitually disregarded.

~Lady Jekyll, D.B.E.

6 ROASTING TO PERFECTION

Roasting, like every other part of the coffee production process, is very complicated and the roaster has to be able to control a huge number of variables. Essentially, roasting is just cooking the beans until they are palatable, but the degree of the roast, and the style of it, can vary considerably, just as the coffee itself can. At its best, roasting can be used to bring out the flavours in the bean. A lighter roast, for example, brings out the citrus and acidic flavours of a coffee, whereas darker roasts (roasted at a higher temperatures) caramelize the natural sugars in the bean and can make the coffee taste sweeter. Roasting usually takes between 10 and 15 minutes, depending on the type of coffee and the roast level required. Longer roasts can 'bake out' any bitter, harsh flavours. Consequently, each batch of coffee is tested and a 'roast profile' is created, detailing the temperature, speed of the roasting machine (coffee is rotated continuously inside the machine) and the time of the ideal roast. Adherence to the roast profile brings out the very best flavours of the coffee (as determined by the expert roasters), essentially showcasing its quality. However, if there is no roast profile, the roaster can damage the coffee by over- or under-roasting it, or simply burning it, and not showing the coffee's true potential.

There is a significant difference again between large scale, commercial roasters, and smaller, more 'artisan' companies. As a rule, larger roasting companies use convection machines, which roast the beans by blasting them with hot air. These machines are computer-controlled, giving far more exact, consistent results by removing the potential for human error. The disadvantage of these machines is that they are designed to roast huge quantities of coffee in one go; (which is also why they are generally used in large commercial companies) but since the quality of the beans can vary so much within an area, a harvest and even within the batch itself, roasting it all at one level leaves no room for this variation. The roast profile would be set according to the 'average' of the coffee, which may not be the best profile for all the batch.

Smaller roasters can use different more 'traditional' machinery such as a Whitmee machine, which is an open-flame roaster. Instead of roasting using hot air, the beans are turned in a drum over an open flame. On average, these machines only roast 70kg of coffee at a time, so unlike the convection roasters, smaller batches can be done without losing any efficiency for the company. This also means that different roast profiles can be designed for each batch of coffee. However, this method requires much more human skill, and therefore, is more prone to mishap. The open-flame machine is manually operated, and the roaster has no controls other than an on-off switch for the gas flame. The roast is controlled entirely by eye – and when it is deemed ready, the flame is extinguished and the coffee is poured out and left to cool. This does give much freedom to work with the variation in the coffee, but when there is just a 2 second difference between excellently roasted coffee and burnt coffee, the margin for error is very slim indeed. Furthermore, with an open-flame, coffee roasted for too long or at too high a temperature, can actually catch fire!

In terms of quality, however, neither method is actually harmful to the coffee or the quality if performed correctly. Instead, the emphasis is more based on the needs of the retailer; coffee shops, cafes and other retailers choose the roaster for pragmatic reasons as well as for perceived quality level. Smaller, independent coffee shops can use smaller roasters because they require less coffee, whilst chain coffee shops with hundreds of stores rely on larger roasting companies so that a regular, consistent supply can be established. The level of consistency required by the retailer does have an effect on the quality as well. As shown before, the roast is not generic, and the style is varied according to the specific coffee batch. Roasting can be used to bring out the unique, subtle nuances of certain coffees, when the variation in taste is taken as a sign of quality. This suits small, independent and often 'gourmet' coffee shops that have the option of stocking a small range of very different coffees, but is not suitable for large companies who need their coffee to taste the same in each store across the world.

The Skilled Palate

Before coffee can be sold, its quality has to be assessed using a method known as cupping. Coffee is sampled by specially trained cuppers, and graded according to its fragrance (of the roasted beans), aroma (of the brewed coffee), body, acidity and aftertaste, and this assessment is used to negotiate the price of the batch of coffee with international buyers. Cupping itself – the ability to distinguish distinct aromas and flavours within a cup of coffee, and then to meaningfully compare it with other batches - is a very unusual skill and takes a long time to learn. Most cuppers practice and learn for over a decade.

El Banco de Olores, or 'smell bank' at Solcafe cupping laboratory, Matagalpa, Nicaragua

Although some people naturally have a better sense of smell than others, a significant part of the cuppers' skill has to be taught and learned, using specialist equipment. El Banco de Olores, or 'smell bank' (often called La Nez du Cafe as well) is the equipment used by professional coffee cuppers to train their sense of smell (and indirectly their palates, as perception of smell and taste are so strongly linked) to help develop their abilities to detect the different, subtle aromas and flavours in the coffees they cup. Each bank comprises of 36 numbered oils infused with different fragrances, ranging from very acrid, unpleasant smells to sharp citruses, pleasant but subtle spice and overpoweringly sweet aromas.

The range was designed by the Speciality Coffee Association of America to include every possible fragrance or combination of fragrances found in roasted coffees. Consistency is maintained as far as possible by every SCAA cupping laboratory having the same set of fragranced oils.

Cupping training is very simple to describe but very difficult to achieve. Trainee cuppers are simply required to smell the oils and learn which smell is which. When they detect these smells in a coffee, they can then refer to the particular number or name of the oil, information which is used to determine the quality of the coffee. However, the presence of unpleasant smells in the coffee does not necessarily mean the coffee is low quality; if for example strong vinegar or coffee-berry scents are detected, this suggests a light-bodied, acidic coffee which is often highly prized commercially. A sweet, caramel flavour on the other hand, can mean the coffee is over-fermented and hence of lower quality.

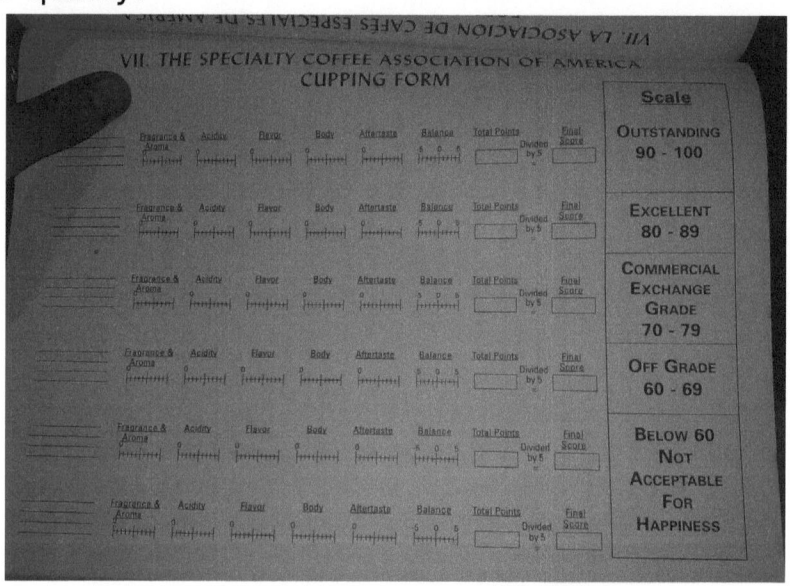

After correctly memorising the whole smell bank, cuppers then learn to detect far more subtle versions of the individual scents in amongst the general aroma of the fresh coffee. The smell bank contains oils infused with the fragrance of chocolate, blackcurrant and vanilla, wood smoke and black pepper, just as can be found in some wines. However, it also contains the smell of potato peelings, milk-whey and molasses, none of which tend to find themselves in the luxurious descriptions on gourmet coffee packaging.

7 THE ART OF THE BARISTA

"Brewing espresso...unlike other methods of brewing coffee...IS rocket science..."

~Kevin Knox and Julie Sheldon Huffaker

(Coffee Basics: A Quick and Easy Guide)

7: THE ART OF THE BARISTA

Making great espresso means knowing the espresso machine very well indeed.

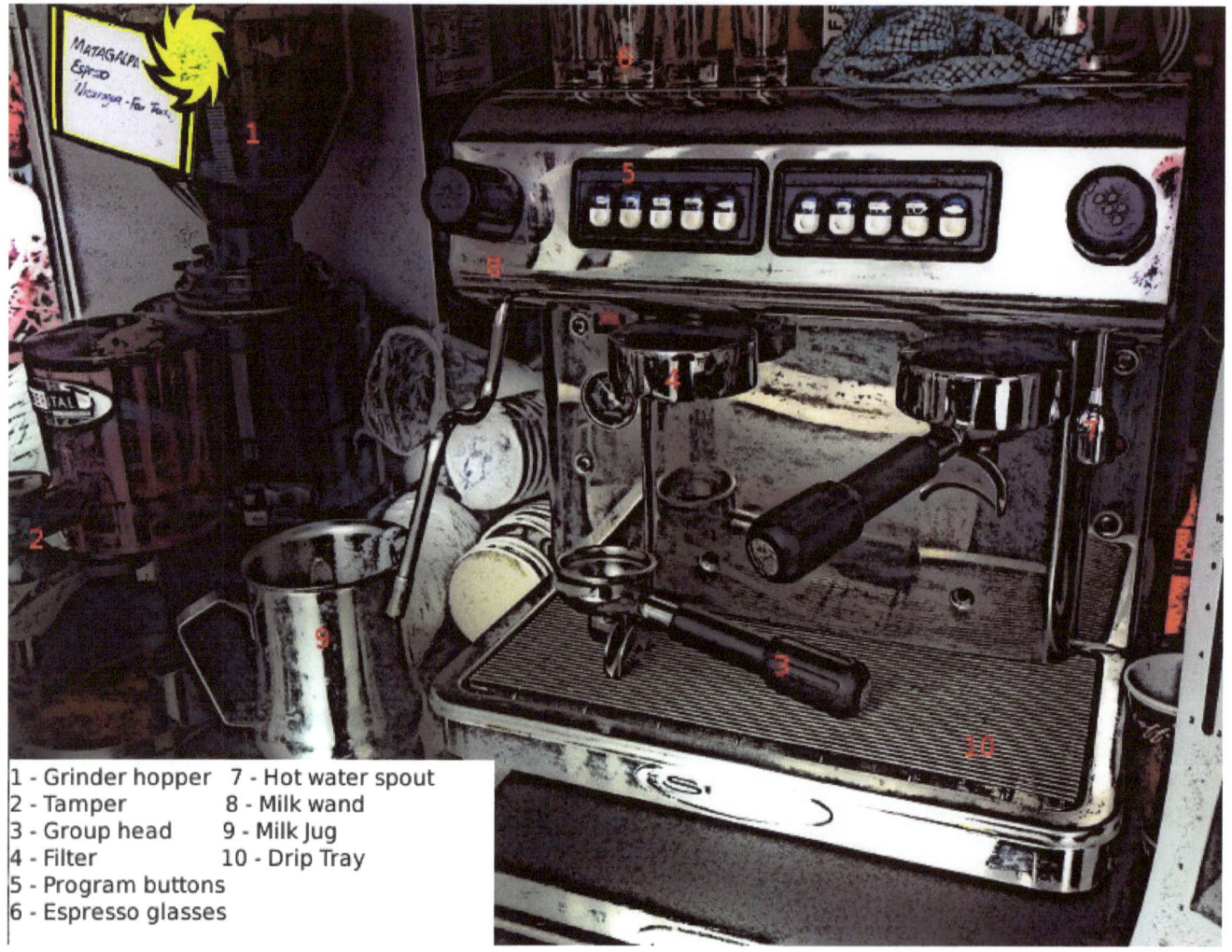

1 - Grinder hopper   7 - Hot water spout
2 - Tamper   8 - Milk wand
3 - Group head   9 - Milk Jug
4 - Filter   10 - Drip Tray
5 - Program buttons
6 - Espresso glasses

This is a small, 2 group commercial espresso machine.

By the time the coffee product arrives at coffee shops, it has already been transformed by several different processes; the physical appearance of coffee has changed significantly from the bright red fruit to roasted hard brown beans. It has also become recognisably COFFEE!

The final stage of transforming the seeds of a tropical plant into a luxury beverage lies in the skills of the barista. The fresh, roasted coffee beans are first ground in a special coffee grinder to a fine powder. Different sorts of coffee grind down differently, and so the barista or coffee shop manager has to experiment at first to calibrate the machine correctly. The grind level can be altered by the barista, making it coarser or finer, depending on the coffee. The coarser the grind, the faster the water will pass through the coffee and the weaker the extracted espresso will become, and the barista has to be sufficiently skilled to know when alterations are needed.

Next, the correct dose must be added to the 'group head' of the espresso machine. The standard dose for a single espresso shot is 7g of ground coffee, although this does vary depending on the grind level and the type of coffee being served. In many places, a double shot, 14g, is used as standard unless the customer requests otherwise. After dosing, the barista has to tamp the coffee correctly, compacting the grounds so that the water is pushed through at the correct speed. Too fast and the espresso is underextracted, weak and bitter. Too slow, and the coffee is thick, strong and burnt. There is no way of mechanically tamping coffee, this task has to be performed by the skilled barista. Most baristas have their own tamper, a favoured and often fetishised object!

If the grind, dose and tamp are right, you should be able to knock out neat little pucks of coffee from the filter handle. They look like little coffee cookies!

The espresso machine is then used to force hot water through the tamped dose of ground coffee; the coffee grounds remain in the group head filter, and the resulting liquid forms the extracted espresso. The espresso machine is programmed in advance and the temperature of the water is usually set around 95 degrees Celsius, 30ml of water is pushed through under at least 15 bars of pressure. The barista can check if the coffee was ground, dosed and tamped correctly by timing the speed of the pour – a good quality espresso should take around 20-25 seconds to pour, and should look like honey dripping off a spoon. However, in Spanish, they call it "collares de raton" - it looks like mouse tails!

The final stage is adding the milk to make the perfect cappuccino or other coffee drink. Fresh milk has to be steamed so that it is hot, thick and textured with microbubbles of air. This is done by using the steam wand on the espresso machine to force steam through the milk in a steel jug. Although the espresso machine controls the pressure and temperature of the steam, texturing milk correctly is a difficult skill to learn, and baristas have to be taught to do this well.

This skill forms the basis of 'latte art' – that is, drawing patterns on the top of the coffee by altering the way the white milk rests on top of the brown espresso crema. There are now national and international competitions for latte art where participants compete to make the best tasting, but also the best presented, coffees.

Latte Art

8 COFFEE COMMUNITIES

Over second and third cups flow matters of high finance, high state, common gossip and low comedy. [Coffee] is a social binder, a warmer of tongues, a soberer of minds, a stimulant of wit, a foiler of sleep if you want it so. From roadside mugs to the classic demi-tasse, it is the perfect democrat.

~The New York Times, 1949

8 COFFEE COMMUNITIES

Walk around any town centre in the UK, and you will find at least one branch of the three big coffee shop chains: Starbucks, Costa Coffee and Caffe Nero, and, with any luck, there might be a few home grown, independent places as well. All three chains have their own set of loyal fans, as do the independents. They may all have one thing in common as well: "Italianess"! Caffe Nero claims it serves "The best espresso this side of Milan." Costa Coffee is "Italian about Coffee", and even Starbucks' CEO, Howard Shultz repeatedly says that he was inspired by the espresso bars he saw on a visit to Italy. This Italianess has produced the psuedo-Italian coffee lingo: "latte" instead of "milky coffee", "grande" and "venti" instead of Large and Extra Large, and even "panini" rather than "toasted sandwich".   In reality, Caffe Nero is a chain based entirely in the UK and its CEO is from California, Costa Coffee is now owned by a British brewery company, Whitbread PLC, and Starbucks has (perhaps unwittingly) become a symbol of America – and also, of capitalism. In fact, none of them now have any real Italian credentials.

An "Italian" independent coffee shop in Sheffield, and Caffe Nero's marketing campaign

So why Italy? It is the Italianess that is the 'unique' selling point. Italianess is part of the 'coffee experience' which the big brands are so keen to promote. Caffe Nero, for instance, want to offer the experience of a old fashioned Italian espresso bar and continental cafe. It gives the coffee, and this 'experience' an identity, which is very important to the brand. Being 'Italian' makes the place sound sophisticated and if not exotic, then certainly different to 'quaint' English tea rooms. It also adds an element of performance. Espresso was invented and perfected in Italy, the first espresso machines were designed and patented by Italians. This style also happens to require more skilled human input, more visual techniques and as such, more labour. Increasing the labour involved increases the value of the end-product, the customer perceives it to be of better quality entirely because it looks more difficult to do, and so espresso coffees become more expensive. The independent coffee shops have picked up on this trend and some even parody it, such as 'Puccinos' who sported the slogan:

"**Pretending to be Italian since 1995**"

It is an often forgotten fact that in the 1950s, Britain had dozens of Italian-style espresso bars, frequented by the young and hip – mainly teenagers who wanted to socialise but were not allowed into bars and pubs. The coffee shops were the place to see and be seen, and drinking coffee was very much a fashion statement. In these respects at least, coffee shops have come full-circle.

It is certainly not just the coffee that keeps people coming to coffee shops and cafes, even if the caffeine is (psychologically) addictive! Coffee shops offer a safe, social environment – safer, more socially acceptable and open to all, unlike pubs and bars. They often provide a useful place somewhere for teenagers to hang around in when they have nothing to do and want to get out of the house! Here in Canada, Tim Hortons coffee shops stay open until late at night, and groups of people are still sat in them, drinking coffee long after everywhere else has closed. In this sense, coffee shops have replaced youth groups and social clubs as the social space of choice.

Starbucks tries to market itself as "the third place" - suitable for working in like your office, but comfortable and friendly like your own home, the coffee shop is somewhere in between. Many places establish themselves in this manner, offering newspapers, big comfy armchairs as well as more formal tables, and also wifi services for people visiting with laptops. Many also offer free or discounted refills and loyalty cards, and all this combines to encourage people to stay there all day. Indeed, many freelancers and people who work from 'home' often use coffee shops to conduct their business from, and are affectionately known as 'cofficers'.

Joining up the coffee world

Coffee shops are also a great place to meet people, socialise, strike up conversations with strangers, and even just to people-watch, but this is far removed from the coffee farming communities in the tropics. The aim of this book was to introduce coffee enthusiasts to the other side of the coffee world – where the beans actually come from and what has to be done to them to transform them into your favourite lattes. The coffee beans have an amazing and complicated journey across the world, and many, many people are involved in the coffee making process. It is an inescapable fact that coffee is produced predominantly in the Third world, but consumed in the First world. But those farmers and producers do not have to be so distant.

The Fairtrade Foundation has done a lot to raise awareness of the conditions in impoverished coffee farming communities, and the more the customers in coffee shops know about where their drink comes from, the stronger the connection with the coffee farmers. Fairtrade is an alternative trade system, designed to offer a guaranteed minimum price for coffee, and protect the farmers from price crashes in the global market. There are a lot of flaws in this system, not least when the global price exceeds the Fairtrade minimum, as it has done for the past few years, leaving farmers who were locked in to Fairtrade contracts unable to sell their crops for the higher market value, and the organisation has come under considerable criticism for this and other aspects of its certification policies. The Fairtrade Foundation has now updated its rules to force buyers to pay the Fairtrade minimum, or the global market price, *whichever is higher,* which has alleviated the situation somewhat, but nevertheless, the Foundation was very slow to react to changing market conditions.

A better economic alternative to Fairtrade is Direct Trade, where the coffee companies go directly to the coffee farms to buy their coffee without employing importing companies. This means that the farmers receive a much larger share of the price of their coffee, as it cuts out the expensive 'middlemen'. However, this is not a practical option for small coffee companies and individual coffee shop owners. It also forgoes the other benefits of the Fairtrade system: the social premium paid to Fairtrade cooperatives, that funds community development projects for example, all of which improves the quality of life for the farmer on top of the fairer price they receive.

So, we are left with coffee drinkers in the UK sitting in pseudo-Italian coffee bars, owned by Americans, and drinking coffee grown in Central and South America, or Africa, or Asia... Or Canadians sitting in cafes named after a dead hockey player, sipping drip coffee of indeterminate origin and wondering whether they ought to be buying Fairtrade coffee instead... The cappuccinos may be delicious, but so few connect the hot, thick brown liquid with the bright red fruit growing high up in the tropical cloud forests. This does not sound like a particularly 'joined up' community.

However, the one thing that unites everyone involved in this 'coffee journey' is a love for the beautiful beans. Coffee inspires passion; the caffeine stimulates the brain, encourages creativity and is a catalyst for good conversations. Next time you enjoy a cup, take a moment to think about where those beans have come from, and the sheer amount of work that has gone in to creating that little bit of luxury. You may enjoy it all the more!

ABOUT THE AUTHOR

Behind every successful woman is a substantial amount of coffee.

~Stephanie Piro

Annabel Townsend has been working in the coffee industry since 2006, and completed a PhD in Human Geography at the University of Sheffield, UK, in 2011. Her research focused on concepts of quality in the speciality coffee industry. She conducted part of a her research at coffee cooperatives in northern Nicaragua and Costa Rica and also in several coffee shops an and roasting companies in the UK. She opened her first coffee business, 'Doctor Coffee's Cafe' in 2009, but moved to Saskatchewan, Canada in 2012 and is still working in the coffee industry. Her first academic book, "Spilling the Beans" was published in October 2012.

RECOMMENDED READING

Brandon, D., 2007 *Life in a 17th Century Coffee Shop* Sutton Publications: London

Ellis, M., 2004 *The Coffee House, a Cultural History.* Phoenix Publications: London

Kuhl, E., 2004 *Nicaragua y Su Cafe* HISPAMER: Managua

Laurier, E., and Philo, C., 2005 *The Cappuccino Community: Cafes and civic life in the contemporary city.* ESRC Research Project: University of Glasgow

Morris, J., and Baldoli, C. 2008 The Cappuccino Conquests: the transnational history of Italian coffee. Retrieved from www.cappuccinoconquests.org.uk

O'Brien, T.G., and Kinnaird, M., 2003 Caffeine and Conservation *Science 300 (5619) 587-588*

Townsend, A., 2012 *Spilling the Beans: Concepts of Quality in the Speciality Coffee Industry* Lambert Academic Press: Berlin

Wild, A., 2004 *Black Gold, a Dark History of Coffee* Harper Perennial: London

For more coffee talk, check out the author's blog at http://drcoffee.wordpress.com

www.ingramcontent.com/pod-product-compliance
Lightning Source LLC
Chambersburg PA
CBHW041512280526
45792CB00004B/1225